Tennessee Cookbook

From Nashville to Memphis Enjoy Authentic Southern Cooking with 50 Delicious Tennessee Recipes

By
BookSumo Press
All rights reserved

Published by
http://www.booksumo.com

ENJOY THE RECIPES?
KEEP ON COOKING WITH 6 MORE FREE COOKBOOKS!

Visit our website and simply enter your email address to join the club and receive your 6 cookbooks.

http://booksumo.com/magnet

 https://www.instagram.com/booksumopress/

 https://www.facebook.com/booksumo/

LEGAL NOTES

All Rights Reserved. No Part Of This Book May Be Reproduced Or Transmitted In Any Form Or By Any Means. Photocopying, Posting Online, And / Or Digital Copying Is Strictly Prohibited Unless Written Permission Is Granted By The Book's Publishing Company. Limited Use Of The Book's Text Is Permitted For Use In Reviews Written For The Public.

Table of Contents

Southern 3-Cheese Spinach 7

Chattanooga Chicken 8

3 Star Carrots 9

Memphis Crock Pot 10

Johnson Family Cornbread 11

Nashville Family Farm Soy Milk 12

Apple Cider Salad 13

Memphis Style BBQ Sauce 14

Tennessee Ceviche 15

Nashville Breakfast 16

Verna's Corn Cakes 17

Big Cypress Sauce 18

How to Fry Catfish 19

Mason Dixon Cake 20

Weeping Willow Coleslaw 22

Nashville Buttermilk Pie 23

Beale Street Sloppy Joes 24

4-Ingredient Tennessee Chicken Cutlets 25

Cookout Steaks 26

Cedars of Lebanon Lasagna 27

Authentic Tennessee Stuffing 28

Deep Fried 'Matoes 29

How to Fry a Chicken 30

Simple Tennessee Porch Tea 31

Fish Cakes 32

Marybelle's Cornbread 33

Backroad Buttery Sweet Potatoes 34

Cracker Crusted Baked Chicken 35

Handmade Breakfast Muffins 36

Dove's Cove Potatoes 37

Tennessee Tilapia 38

BBQ Sirloin Nashville Style 39

Catfish Lunch Box 40

Tennessee Mac and Cheese 41

How to Make Collard Greens 42

Sweet Onions and Okra 43

Black Bean Shoe Peg Salad 44

Fresh Blueberry Iced Tea 45

Chicken Tenders Tennessee Style 46

How to Make Black-Eyed Peas 47

Simply Corn Fried 48

Buttermilk Cornbread 49

Chickasaw Greens 50

Real Southern Macaroni and Cheese 51

Red White and Blue Patty 52

Easy Jalapeno Bites 53

Pinto Beans Tennessee 54

Sweet Honey Chicken 55

Authentic Southern Corn 56

Sweet Honey Chicken 57

Southern 3-Cheese Spinach

🥣 Prep Time: 30 mins
🕐 Total Time: 45 mins

Servings per Recipe: 12
Calories 384.8
Fat 27.5g
Cholesterol 84.3mg
Sodium 710.5mg
Carbohydrates 15.1g
Protein 21.5g

Ingredients

- 5 (10 oz.) packages frozen chopped spinach
- 4 1/2 C. milk
- 1 tsp dry mustard
- 1 tsp garlic powder
- 1 1/2 tsp crushed red pepper flakes
- 1/2 medium yellow onion, chopped
- 1 tbsp butter
- 5 tbsp melted butter
- 6 tbsp flour
- 8 oz. Velveeta cheese (cubed)
- 8 oz. cheddar cheese (cubed)
- 4 oz. monterey jack cheese (cubed)
- 1 1/2 C. grated monterey jack cheese, for topping

Directions

1. Set your oven to 350 degrees F before doing anything else.
2. Thaw the frozen spinach and squeeze the water completely.
3. In a 4 quart pan, add the milk and spices on medium heat and heat to just below a boil.
4. Reduce the heat and simmer.
5. In a skillet, melt 1 tbsp of the butter on medium heat and sauté the onion for about 5-8 minutes.
6. Transfer the onion into the milk mixture.
7. In a small pan, mix together 5 tbsp of the melted butter and flour on low heat and cook for about 2-3 minutes, stirring continuously.
8. Transfer the flour into the milk mixture and stir to combine.
9. Cook till the sauce becomes thick.
10. Add the cubed cheeses and cook till the cheese melts completely and blended into the sauce.
11. Remove from the heat and keep aside to cool for about 15 minutes.
12. Add the spinach and mix till well combined.
13. Transfer the mixture into a large casserole dish and sprinkle with the grated Monterey Jack cheese.
14. Cook in the oven for about 12-15 minutes.

CHATTANOOGA
Chicken

🥣 Prep Time: 25 mins
🕐 Total Time: 1 hr 5 mins

Servings per Recipe: 6
Calories 309.1
Fat 5.6g
Cholesterol 68.4mg
Sodium 1210.3mg
Carbohydrates 35.7g
Protein 29.7g

Ingredients

6 boneless skinless chicken breast halves
1 tsp salt
1/4 tsp pepper
1/2 C. flour
1 large onion, chopped
2 tbsp margarine
1 1/2 C. ketchup

4 tbsp lemon juice
2 tsp mustard
4 tbsp light brown sugar
1 tsp Worcestershire sauce
1 C. water

Directions

1. Set your oven to 400 degrees F before doing anything else and grease a 13x9-inch baking dish.
2. Season the chicken with the salt and pepper evenly.
3. Coat the chicken with the flour.
4. In a skillet, heat a little oil and cook the chicken till browned.
5. Place the chicken into the prepared baking dish.
6. In a pan, melt the margarine and sauté the onion till browned.
7. Add the remaining ingredients and simmer for about 15 minutes.
8. Place the mixture over the chicken evenly.
9. Cook in the oven for about 40 minutes.

3 Star Carrots

Prep Time: 10 mins
Total Time: 25 mins

Servings per Recipe: 6
Calories   154.0
Fat   4.2g
Cholesterol   10.1mg
Sodium   135.4mg
Carbohydrates   29.9g
Protein   1.4g

Ingredients

2 lb. carrots, scraped and thinly sliced
1/2 C. water
3 tbsp honey
3 tbsp brown sugar
2 tbsp butter

Directions

1. In a medium a pan, add the carrots and water and bring to a boil.
2. Reduce the heat and simmer, covered for about 8 minutes.
3. Drain the carrots and return to pan.
4. Add honey and remaining ingredients and stir to combine.'
5. Reduce the heat to low and cook till the butter melts completely, stirring gently.

MEMPHIS
Crock Pot

🥣 Prep Time: 15 mins
🕐 Total Time: 10 h 15 m

Servings per Recipe: 6
Calories   479.7
Fat   23.0g
Cholesterol   115.6mg
Sodium   383.3mg
Carbohydrates   30.2g
Protein   38.3g

Ingredients

1 lb stewing beef, cubed
1 lb chicken, cubed
1/4 C. chili powder
1 large green bell pepper, chopped
1 large onion, chopped
1 (6 oz.) cans tomato paste
1/2 C. firmly-packed brown sugar

1/4 C. vinegar
1 tsp dry mustard
1 tsp Worcestershire sauce
salt and pepper

Directions

1. In a crock pot, mix together all the ingredients.
2. Set the crock pot on Low and cook, covered for about 10 hours.

Johnson Family Cornbread

Prep Time: 20 mins
Total Time: 1 hr 20 mins

Servings per Recipe: 1
Calories   1973.2
Fat   41.6g
Cholesterol   292.1mg
Sodium   2989.8mg
Carbohydrates   360.2g
Protein   49.0g

Ingredients

- 2 tbsp butter
- 2 C. white cornmeal
- 1/2 C. all-purpose flour (sifted before measuring)
- 1/2 C. sugar
- 1/2 tsp salt
- 1 tsp baking powder
- 1/2 tsp baking soda
- 2 C. buttermilk
- 1 egg, beaten

Directions

1. Set your oven to 350 degrees F before doing anything else and arrange a rack in the center of the oven.
2. In a 9x5x2-inch loaf pan, place the butter and keep in the oven to melt.
3. In large bowl, sift together the cornmeal, flour, sugar, salt, baking powder and baking soda.
4. Add the buttermilk and egg into the cornmeal mixture.
5. Remove the loaf pan from the oven and transfer the hot melted butter into the cornmeal mixture.
6. Keep the loaf pan aside to cool.
7. With a wooden spoon, mix till the mixture becomes moist.
8. Grease the inside of the cooled loaf pan with the solid vegetable shortening generously.
9. Place the mixture into the prepared loaf pan evenly.
10. Place the loaf pan over the center rack of the oven and cook for about 1 hour or till a toothpick inserted in the center comes out clean.
11. Remove from the oven and immediately, invert onto the wire rack to cool for about 5 minute.
12. Cut into thick slices and serve.

NASHVILLE FAMILY
Farm Soy Milk

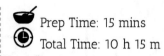

Prep Time: 15 mins
Total Time: 10 h 15 m

Servings per Recipe: 6
Calories   148.7
Fat   7.7g
Cholesterol   0.0mg
Sodium   7.9mg
Carbohydrates   8.5g
Protein   14.3g

Ingredients
2 1/2 C. whole soybeans
5 C. cool water

Directions
1. Rinse 2-1/2 C. of the whole soybeans.
2. In a large bowl, add 5 C. of the cool water and soak the whole soybeans for about 8-10 hours.
3. In a bowl, add 1 C. of the soybeans with 2-1/2 C. of the hot water and with an electric mixer, beat at high speed for about 1 minute.
4. Repeat with the remaining soybeans.
5. In a large pan, add the soybeans on medium-high heat and bring to a boil.
6. Reduce the heat and simmer for about 20 minutes, stirring occasionally.
7. Strain the soybeans through a cheesecloth, twisting pulp in cloth to squeeze out the milk.
8. Repeat the process, pouring 2 C. of the boiling water in with remaining pulp and straining again.

Apple Cider Salad

Prep Time: 15 mins
Total Time: 2 hr 15 mins

Servings per Recipe: 1
Calories	166.0
Fat	0.8g
Cholesterol	0.0mg
Sodium	273.5mg
Carbohydrates	37.6g
Protein	6.6g

Ingredients

- 1/2 head red cabbage
- 1/4 C. apple cider vinegar
- 3 tbsp fresh lemon juice
- 1/4 tsp onion powder
- 1/4 tsp garlic powder
- 1 garlic clove, minced
- 1 tbsp onion, finely chopped
- 1 dash cayenne pepper
- 4 drops stevia
- 1 dash sea salt
- 1 dash pepper

Directions

1. Slice the cabbage thinly and keep aside.
2. In a large bowl, mix together the remaining ingredients.
3. Add the cabbage and mix well.
4. Refrigerate to chill for at least 1-2 hours.

MEMPHIS STYLE
BBQ Sauce

Prep Time: 40 mins
Total Time: 1 hr 25 m

Servings per Recipe: 1
Calories 581.0
Fat 6.3g
Cholesterol 0.0mg
Sodium 5581.3mg
Carbohydrates 130.0g
Protein 6.7g

Ingredients
1 tbsp olive oil
1/2 onion, diced
2 garlic cloves, smashed and minced
4 C. ketchup
1/2 C. water
2 C. distilled white vinegar
1/2 C. Worcestershire sauce

1/2 C. packed light brown sugar
1 tbsp dry mustard
1 tbsp crushed red pepper flakes
2 tsp sea salt
1/2 tsp fresh ground black pepper
1/2 lemon, cut in half

Directions
1. In a large pan, heat the oil on medium heat and sauté the onion for about 5 minutes.
2. Add the garlic and sauté for about 1 minute.
3. Stir in the ketchup.
4. Fill the bottle of ketchup with the water and add it to the pan, stirring to combine.
5. Add the vinegar, Worcestershire sauce, brown sugar, mustard, red pepper flakes, salt and black pepper and stir to combine.
6. Squeeze the lemon juice into the sauce.
7. Stir in the squeezed halves and bring the sauce to a gentle boil.
8. Reduce the heat and simmer for about 45 minutes, stirring occasionally.
9. Remove from the heat and keep aside to cool slightly.
10. Discard the lemon halves.
11. Transfer into an airtight container and refrigerate till using.
12. This sauce can be preserved in refrigerator for up to 3 weeks.

Tennessee Ceviche

Prep Time: 8 hr
Total Time: 8 hr

Servings per Recipe: 8	
Calories	100.7
Fat	0.9g
Cholesterol	0.0mg
Sodium	362.2mg
Carbohydrates	20.9g
Protein	4.7g

Ingredients

1 (15 oz.) cans black-eyed peas, drained
1 (11 oz.) cans corn, drained
1 medium tomatoes, chopped
1 medium green pepper, chopped
2 -4 green onions, sliced
1/3 C. chopped fresh cilantro
1 C. picante sauce
2 tbsp cider vinegar
2 garlic cloves, minced

Directions

1. In a bowl, mix together all the ingredients and refrigerate to chill for about 8 hours.
2. Drain and serve.

NASHVILLE
Breakfast

Prep Time: 25 mins
Total Time: 1 hr 25 m

Servings per Recipe: 6
Calories 1442.0
Fat 109.3g
Cholesterol 239.3mg
Sodium 2771.9mg
Carbohydrates 58.7g
Protein 52.8g

Ingredients

2 lb. Italian turkey sausage
2 C. shredded cheddar cheese
1 (10 3/4 oz.) cans cream of chicken soup
1 C. sour cream
1 (8 oz.) containers French onion dip
1 C. onion, chopped
1/4 C. green bell pepper
1/4 C. red bell pepper
salt and pepper
1 (30 oz.) hash brown potatoes, shredded, thawed

Directions

1. Set your oven to 350 degrees F before doing anything else and grease a 13x9-inch baking dish.
2. Heat a large skillet and cook the sausage till browned completely.
3. Drain the excess grease from the skillet.
4. In a large bowl, add the cheese, chicken soup, sour cream, French onion dip, onion, bell peppers, salt and pepper and mix till well combined.
5. Fold in the thawed hash brown potatoes.
6. Spread 1/2 of the hash brown mixture in the prepared baking dish and top with half of the cooked sausage.
7. Repeat the layers.
8. Cook in the oven for about 1 hour.

Verna's Corn Cakes

Prep Time: 10 mins
Total Time: 13 mins

Servings per Recipe: 6
Calories	181.3
Fat	9.2g
Cholesterol	39.5mg
Sodium	31.0mg
Carbohydrates	18.5g
Protein	7.6g

Ingredients

Bean Salsa:
- 1 tbsp crisco vegetable oil
- 1/2 C. chopped onion
- 1 garlic clove, minced
- 1 (15 1/2 oz.) cans great northern beans, drained
- 1 medium tomatoes, seeded and chopped
- 1 small jalapeno chile, minced
- 1/2 avocado, finely chopped
- 1/2 C. chopped bell pepper
- 2 tbsp chopped fresh cilantro
- 1 tbsp lemon juice
- salt and pepper, to taste

Cakes:
- 1 large egg
- 1 C. Martha White self-rising corn meal mix (white)
- 1/2 tsp sugar
- 3/4 C. milk
- 1 tbsp crisco vegetable oil

Directions

1. For the corn cakes in a large bowl, add the egg and beat well.
2. Add the corn meal mix, sugar and milk and mix well.
3. Heat a lightly greased large skillet on medium heat.
4. Add 1/4 C. of the mixture and cook till the edges look cooked and bubbles begin to appear on surface from both sides.
5. Repeat with the remaining mixture.
6. In a medium pan, heat the oil on medium heat and sauté the onion and garlic for about 5 minutes.
7. Stir in the beans and cook till bubbly.
8. With a potato masher, mash the mixture till thick and lumpy.
9. Transfer the mixture into serving bowl.
10. For the salsa in a bowl, mix together all ingredients.
11. Place the salsa over the bean mixture and serve with the corn cakes.

BIG
Cypress Sauce

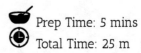
Prep Time: 5 mins
Total Time: 25 m

Servings per Recipe: 4
Calories 254.0
Fat 0.6g
Cholesterol 0.0mg
Sodium 772.6mg
Carbohydrates 62.9g
Protein 1.8g

Ingredients
1/2 C. sugar
1/2 C. brown sugar
1/2 C. ketchup
1/2 C. finely chopped onion
1/4 C. white vinegar

1/4 C. mustard
1 tbsp soy sauce
1 tbsp garlic salt

Directions
1. In a pan, add all the ingredients and bring to a boil.
2. Reduce the heat to low and simmer for about 20 minutes, stirring occasionally.
3. Coat the meat with the sauce ,while baking or grilling, turning meat occasionally.

How to Fry Catfish

Prep Time: 15 mins
Total Time: 15 mins

Servings per Recipe: 6
Calories   136.0
Fat   1.3g
Cholesterol   0.0mg
Sodium   894.7mg
Carbohydrates   28.6g
Protein   3.3g

Ingredients

6 small catfish
1 tsp salt
1/4 tsp pepper

2 C. self-rising cornmeal
corn oil

Directions

1. Season the catfish with the salt and pepper evenly.
2. In a paper bag, place the cornmeal.
3. Add the catfish, 1 at a time and shake the bag to coat completely.
4. In a deep pan, heat the oil and deep fry the catfish in batches till golden brown.
5. With a slotted spoon, transfer the catfish onto a paper towel lined plate to drain.
6. Serve hot.

MASON DIXON Cake

Prep Time: 30 mins
Total Time: 1 hr 10 m

Servings per Recipe: 12
Calories 783.9
Fat 38.2g
Cholesterol 64.8mg
Sodium 135.3mg
Carbohydrates 104.6g
Protein 11.3g

Ingredients

2 C. all-purpose flour
1/2 tsp baking soda
1/2 C. vegetable shortening
1 1/2 C. sugar
2 eggs
2 ripe bananas
1/4 C. buttermilk
1 tsp pure vanilla extract

1 C. walnut
Cake Topping:
1/2 C. butter, softened
1 C. packed dark brown sugar
1/3 C. heavy cream
1 tbsp pure vanilla extract
1 (16 oz.) boxes confectioners' sugar
2 C. finely chopped walnuts

Directions

1. Set your oven to 450 degrees F before doing anything else and grease and flour 2(9-inch) cake pans.
2. For the cake in a bowl, mix together the flour and baking soda.
3. In another bowl, add the shortening and sugar and with an electric mixer, beat till light and fluffy.
4. Add eggs, 1 at a time and mix well.
5. Add the mashed bananas, buttermilk and vanilla and mix well.
6. Add the flour mixture and mix till just combined.
7. Fold in the walnuts.
8. Divide the mixture into the prepared pans evenly.
9. Cook in the oven for about 35 minutes or till a toothpick inserted in the center comes out clean.
10. Remove from the oven and keep onto the wire rack to cool in the pans for about 5-10 minutes.
11. Carefully, invert the cakes onto the wire rack to cool completely.
12. For the frosting in a small pan, melt the butter on medium-low heat and cook the brown sugar and 1/3 C. of the cream for about 2 minutes, stirring continuously.

13. Remove from the heat and stir in the vanilla.
14. Transfer the mixture into a large bowl.
15. Slowly, add the confectioners sugar a little at a time and with a hand mixer, beat till smooth.
16. With a small spatula, cover the top of one cake with some frosting.
17. Place second cake layer on top and press gently to make it level.
18. Spread the remaining frosting on top and sides of assembled cake evenly.
19. Press chopped walnuts on sides of cake.

WEEPING
Willow Coleslaw

Prep Time: 30 mins
Total Time: 45 mins

Servings per Recipe: 8
Calories   198.0
Fat   7.5g
Cholesterol   0.0mg
Sodium   904.9mg
Carbohydrates   32.5g
Protein   3.2g

Ingredients

3/4 C. sugar
1/4 C. vegetable oil
1/4 C. cider vinegar
1 tbsp salt
1 tsp black pepper, coarsely ground
1 tbsp dry mustard
1 tsp celery seed
1 green pepper, seeded and finely sliced

3 lb. cabbage, shredded
2 medium onions, finely sliced

Directions

1. In a pan, add the sugar, oil, vinegar, salt, pepper, dry mustard and celery seed and bring to a boil.
2. Remove from the heat and stir the mixture well.
3. In a glass bowl, place the green peppers, cabbage and onions.
4. Place the dressing over the salad.
5. Refrigerate, covered for about 24 hours before serving.

Nashville Buttermilk Pie

🥣 Prep Time: 15 mins
🕐 Total Time: 1 hr

Servings per Recipe: 1
Calories   3282.1
Fat   184.8g
Cholesterol   637.7mg
Sodium   1954.6mg
Carbohydrates   383.0g
Protein   40.7g

Ingredients

1 8 inch unbaked pie crust
3 eggs, beaten
1/4 C. margarine
1 1/3 C. sugar
1 tbsp flour
1 pinch salt
1/3 C. buttermilk
1 tsp vinegar
1 (3 1/2 oz.) cans coconut

Directions

1. Set your oven to 350 degrees F before doing anything else.
2. In a bowl, add the butter and sugar and beat till creamy.
3. Add the remaining ingredients and mix till well combined.
4. Arrange the pie crust into a pie dish.
5. Place the mixture into th pie crust evenly.
6. Cook in the oven for about 45 minutes.
7. Remove from the oven and keep aside to cool completely before serving.

BEALE STREET
Sloppy Joes

Prep Time: 5 mins
Total Time: 15 mins

Servings per Recipe: 6
Calories   207.2
Fat   14.3g
Cholesterol   50.6mg
Sodium   367.9mg
Carbohydrates   3.4g
Protein   15.3g

Ingredients
1 lb. 90/10 ground sirloin
1 can cream of mushroom soup

Directions
1. Heat a large skillet and cook the ground sirloin till browned completely.
2. Drain the excess grease from the skillet.
3. Add the mushroom soup and simmer, covered for about 5-7 minutes.

4-Ingredient Tennessee Chicken Cutlets

Prep Time: 8 mins
Total Time: 28 mins

Servings per Recipe: 4
Calories	236.6
Fat	2.6g
Cholesterol	68.4mg
Sodium	255.3mg
Carbohydrates	24.2g
Protein	28.4g

Ingredients
- 1/4 C. honey
- 2 tbsp prepared mustard
- 1/2 C. saltine crumbs
- 4 boneless skinless chicken breast halves

Directions
1. Set your oven to 400 degrees F before doing anything else and lightly, grease a baking sheet with the cooking spray.
2. In a bowl, mix together the honey and mustard.
3. Reserve about 2 tbsp of honey mixture in a small bowl.
4. In a shallow dish, spread the crumbs.
5. Dip the chicken breast halves in honey mixture and then coat with the crumbs evenly.
6. Arrange the chicken breast halves onto the prepared baking sheet.
7. Cook in the oven for about 18-20 minutes.
8. Serve the chicken with a drizzling of the reserved honey mixture.

COOKOUT
Steaks

🥣 Prep Time: 40 mins
🕐 Total Time: 2 hr

Servings per Recipe: 4
Calories   676.2
Fat   45.4g
Cholesterol   183.7mg
Sodium   808.9mg
Carbohydrates   13.2g
Protein   47.5g

Ingredients

Topping:
1/2 C. ketchup
2 tbsp broth
1 tbsp steak sauce
1 tbsp dark brown sugar
2 tsp Worcestershire sauce
1/4 tsp granulated garlic
1/4 tsp kosher salt
1/4 tsp fresh ground black pepper

Meat:
4 (8 oz.) New York strip steaks (1 inch thick)
3 medium garlic cloves
1/2 tsp kosher salt
3 tbsp extra virgin olive oil
1 tbsp finely chopped fresh rosemary
2 tsp fresh coarse ground black pepper

Directions

1. Trim most of the exterior fat from the steaks and keep in the room temperature for about 20-30 minutes before the grilling.
2. Set your grill for high heat and grease the grill grate.
3. For the sauce in a small pan, add all the ingredients and 1/2 C. of the water on medium-high heat and beat till well combined.
4. Bring to a boil, stirring occasionally.
5. Reduce the heat and simmer for about 10 minutes, stirring occasionally.
6. Roughly chop the garlic onto a cutting board and sprinkle with the salt.
7. With the sharp edge and the flat side of the knife blade, crush the garlic and salt till a paste is formed.
8. In a small bowl, mix together the garlic paste, oil, rosemary and pepper.
9. Rub the mixture over the steaks evenly.
10. Cook the steaks on the grill over direct high heat for about 3-4 minutes per side.
11. Remove from the grill and keep aside for about 3-5 minutes.
12. Serve warm alongside the sauce.

Cedars of Lebanon Lasagna

🥣 Prep Time: 30 min
🕐 Total Time: 2 hr

Servings per Recipe: 10
Calories 699.0
Fat 40.4g
Cholesterol 131.3mg
Sodium 662.2mg
Carbohydrates 44.3g
Protein 39.1g

Ingredients

- 1 (16 oz.) packages elbow macaroni
- 1/4 C. butter
- 1 lb sharp cheddar cheese, cut into cubes divided
- 1 C. parmesan cheese
- 1 medium onion, chopped
- 2 garlic cloves, minced
- 1 tbsp oil
- 1 small celery rib, chopped
- 1 green bell pepper, cut into strips
- 2 lb. ground chuck
- 1 tsp chili powder
- 1/4 tsp cumin
- 1 dash oregano
- 8 mushrooms, thinly sliced
- 1 dash Worcestershire sauce
- salt and pepper
- red pepper flakes
- 2 (16 oz.) cans chopped tomatoes
- 1 (8 oz.) cans tomato sauce

Directions

1. Set your oven to 350 degrees F before doing anything else.
2. In a large pan of the lightly salted boiling water, prepare the macaroni according to the package's directions.
3. Drain well.
4. For the sauce in a pan, heat the oil on medium heat and sauté the onion and garlic till browned.
5. Add the celery and green pepper and cook till softened.
6. Transfer the onion mixture into a bowl.
7. In the same pan, add the ground beef and cook till browned completely.
8. Add the onion mixture, salt, pepper, chili powder, cumin, Worcestershire sauce, pinch oregano, mushrooms, red pepper flakes, tomatoes and tomato sauce and stir to combine.
9. Reduce the heat to low and simmer for about 1 hour.
10. In a large casserole dish, place a layer of the cooked macaroni and dot with the butter, followed by add 1/2 of the cheese cubes, a layer of the sauce and sprinkle with the red pepper flakes.
11. Repeat the layers, finishing with the sauce; and sprinkle with the Parmesan cheese.
12. Cook in the oven for about 30 minutes.

AUTHENTIC
Tennessee Stuffing

Prep Time: 20 mins
Total Time: 2 hr 20 mins

Servings per Recipe: 6
Calories 339 kcal
Fat 20.3 g
Carbohydrates 13.8g
Protein 25.4 g
Cholesterol 83 mg
Sodium 273 mg

Ingredients

6 boneless quail, optional
salt to taste
2 tsp grated orange zest, divided
2 1/2 C. vegetable broth
1/2 C. uncooked wild rice
1 bay leaf
1 tbsp vegetable oil
1 C. diced onion

3/4 C. diced celery
1/2 C. fresh sage, minced
1 egg white
1/3 C. toasted walnuts
1/2 tsp freshly ground black pepper
1/4 C. fresh parsley, minced
1/2 C. chicken broth

Directions

1. Set your oven to 375 degrees F before doing anything else and lightly, grease a large roasting pan.
2. Wash the quail completely and with the paper towels, pat dry.
3. Rub the inside cavity of each quail with the salt and 1 tsp of the orange zest.
4. In a medium pan, add the vegetable broth and rice and bring to a boil.
5. Add the bay leaf and stir to combine.
6. Reduce the heat to low and simmer, covered for about 35-40 minutes.
7. Meanwhile in a medium skillet, heat the oil on medium heat and sauté the onions till translucent.
8. Add the celery and sage and sauté for about 2 minutes.
9. Transfer the mixture into a medium bowl.
10. Add the egg white, remaining orange zest, walnuts, black pepper, cooked rice and parsley and mix till well combined.
11. Stuff the cavity of each quail with the rice mixture evenly and sprinkle the skins with the salt and black pepper slightly.
12. Arrange the quail into the prepared roasting pan.
13. Cook in the oven for about 35-40 minutes.
14. Transfer the quail into a serving platter.
15. In the roasting pan, the chicken broth and de glaze completely.
16. Strain the broth and place over the quail before serving.

Deep Fried 'Matoes

Prep Time: 5 min
Total Time: 17 mins

Servings per Recipe: 6
Calories   289 kcal
Fat   10.2 g
Carbohydrates   42.7 g
Protein   6.6 g
Cholesterol   37 mg
Sodium   300 mg

Ingredients
1 extra large egg
4 tbsp milk
1 C. cornmeal
1 C. all-purpose flour
3 tbsp extra virgin olive oil
3 green tomatoes, sliced

Directions
1. In a small bowl, add the egg and milk and beat till well combined.
2. In another small bowl, mix together the cornmeal and flour.
3. Dip the tomato slices in egg mixture and then coat with the cornmeal mixture.
4. In a large skillet, heat the oil on medium heat and cook the tomato slices till browned from both sides.

HOW TO FRY a Chicken

Prep Time: 10 mins
Total Time: 40 mins

Servings per Recipe: 4
Calories 797.0
Fat 39.7g
Cholesterol 356.1mg
Sodium 3012.2mg
Carbohydrates 50.4g
Protein 55.3g

Ingredients
2 lb. cut-up chicken
Sauce:
4 eggs
1/3 C. water
1 C. hot sauce
Spice Mix:
1 1/2 tsp salt
1 1/4 tsp fresh ground black pepper
1/4 tsp garlic powder
Dredge:
2 C. all-purpose flour
1 tbsp baking powder
1/4 tsp salt

Directions
1. For sauce in a bowl, add the eggs and water and beat well.
2. Add the hot sauce and beat till well combined.
3. Transfer the mixture into a large plastic zip-top bag.
4. For seasoning mixture in a small bowl, mix together 1 tsp of the salt, 1/4 tsp of the black pepper and 1/4 tsp of the garlic powder.
5. For dredging mixture in another bowl, mix together the flour, baking powder and 1/4 tsp of the salt.
6. Rinse the chicken pieces and with paper towels, pat dry.
7. Cut the breast pieces in half across the ribs.
8. Season the chicken with the seasoning blend generously on both sides.
9. In the bag of sauce mixture, place the chicken pieces in batches and squish around to coat completely.
10. The, coat the chicken pieces with the flour mixture.
11. In a large deep pan, heat the peanut oil to 350 degrees F and fry the chicken pieces in batches till golden brown and crisp.
12. With a slotted spoon, transfer the chicken onto a paper towel lined plate to drain.

Simple Tennessee Porch Tea

Prep Time: 15 min
Total Time: 30 mins

Servings per Recipe: 1
Calories   580.5
Fat   0.0g
Cholesterol   0.0mg
Sodium   108.6mg
Carbohydrates   149.9g
Protein   0.0g

Ingredients

6 regular tea bags
1/8 tsp baking soda
2 C. boiling water
1 1/2-2 C. sugar
6 C. cold water

Directions

1. In a large glass C., place the tea bags and baking soda.
2. Place the boiling water over the tea bags and steep, covered for about 15 minutes.
3. Remove the tea bags and transfer the tea mixture into a 2-quart pitcher.
4. Add the sugar and stir till the sugar dissolves.
5. Add the cold water and refrigerate to chill completely.
6. Serve the iced tea over more ice.

FISH
Cakes

🥣 Prep Time: 15 mins
🕐 Total Time: 35 mins

Servings per Recipe: 4
Calories 263.1
Fat 10.2g
Cholesterol 135.1mg
Sodium 516.5mg
Carbohydrates 15.4g
Protein 27.3g

Ingredients
1 (14 3/4 oz.) canned salmon
1/4 C. onion, finely chopped
1/4 C. cornmeal
1/4 C. flour
1 egg
3 tbsp mayonnaise

Directions
1. Open the can of the salmon and drain completely.
2. In a bowl, place the salmon and with a fork, flake evenly.
3. Add onion, cornmeal, flour, mayonnaise and egg and mix till well combined.
4. Make equal sized patties from the mixture.
5. In a skillet, heat the oil on medium heat and cook the patties till browned from both sides.

Marybelle's Cornbread

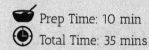
Prep Time: 10 min
Total Time: 35 mins

Servings per Recipe: 8
Calories   235.0
Fat   11.3g
Cholesterol   32.4mg
Sodium   303.3mg
Carbohydrates   29.1g
Protein   4.9g

Ingredients

- 1 C. yellow cornmeal
- 1 C. unbleached all-purpose flour
- 1 tbsp baking powder
- 1/4 tsp salt
- 1/4 tsp baking soda
- 1 1/4 C. buttermilk
- 1 large egg
- 2 tbsp sugar
- 1/4 C. corn oil
- 2 tbsp unsalted butter

Directions

1. Set your oven to 375 degrees F before doing anything else.
2. Place an oven proof skillet in the oven while preheating.
3. In a bowl, mix together the cornmeal, flour, baking powder and salt.
4. In another bowl, mix together the buttermilk and baking soda.
5. In a small bowl, add the egg and sugar beat till well combined.
6. Add the oil and mix till combined.
7. Add the egg mixture into the bowl of the buttermilk mixture and mix till well combined.
8. After the oven is preheated, place the butter into the skillet to melt.
9. Add the egg mixture into the flour mixture and mix till a dough is formed.
10. Remove the skillet from the oven and swirl the skillet to cover the bottom and sides evenly.
11. Immediately, place the flour mixture in the skillet and with the back of the spoon, smoothing the top surface.
12. Cook in the oven for about 25 minutes.
13. Remove from the oven and carefully, invert onto a cutting board.
14. Cut into desired sized wedges and serve.

BACKROAD BUTTERY
Sweet Potatoes

Prep Time: 5 mins
Total Time: 15 mins

Servings per Recipe: 4
Calories 146.8
Fat 3.9g
Cholesterol 10.0mg
Sodium 253.1mg
Carbohydrates 26.5g
Protein 2.1g

Ingredients
4 sweet potatoes
4 tsp butter, divided equally
1/2 tsp cinnamon
1/4 tsp chili powder

1/8 tsp cayenne
1/4 tsp salt

Directions
1. Wash the sweet potatoes and with a fork, prick each one.
2. In a microwave safe bowl, place the sweet potatoes and microwave for about 5-7 minutes.
3. In a bowl, mix together the spices and keep aside.
4. Make a slit in each sweet potato.
5. Insert 1 tsp of the butter into each sweet potato and sprinkle with the spice mixture.
6. With a fork, fluff the flesh of the sweet potato to mix in butter and spices.

Cracker Crusted Baked Chicken

Prep Time: 15 min
Total Time: 50 mins

Servings per Recipe: 4
Calories   1051.5
Fat   87.6g
Cholesterol   294.5mg
Sodium   973.8mg
Carbohydrates   19.7g
Protein   45.6g

Ingredients

- 1 whole broiler-fryer chicken (cut into pieces)
- 1 C. butter (melted)
- 2 C. Ritz crackers (crushed)
- 1 tsp garlic powder
- 1 tsp dried parsley flakes
- 1/4 tsp salt
- 1/2 tsp ground black pepper
- 1/4 tsp paprika
- 1/4 tsp sage
- 1/4 tsp cumin

Directions

1. Set your oven to 400 degrees F before doing anything else and grease a cake style pan.
2. Wash the chicken completely and with the paper towels, pat dry.
3. In a medium bowl, place the melted butter.
4. In a large bowl, place the Ritz cracker crumbs.
5. In a small bowl, mix together all the seasonings.
6. Dip the chicken pieces in the butter and then coat with the cracker crumbs.
7. Arrange the chicken in the prepared pan and sprinkle with the seasoning mixture.
8. Cook in the oven for about 35-45 minute, flipping once in the middle way.

HANDMADE
Breakfast Muffins

 Prep Time: 15 mins
Total Time: 35 mins

Servings per Recipe: 1
Calories 222.6
Fat 12.5g
Cholesterol 33.3mg
Sodium 228.3mg
Carbohydrates 24.3g
Protein 3.4g

Ingredients
2 1/2 C. all-purpose flour
3 tbsp sugar
1 1/2 tbsp baking powder
3/4 C. cold butter
1 C. cold milk

Directions
1. Set your oven to 400 degrees F before doing anything else and grease 12 cups of a muffin pan.
2. In large bowl, mix together the flour, sugar and baking powder.
3. With a pastry cutter, cut the butter till a coarse crumb like mixture is formed.
4. Add the milk and with a fork, mix till the mixture becomes moist.
5. Transfer the mixture into the prepared muffin cups evenly.
6. Cook in the oven for about 20 minutes.
7. Remove from the oven and keep onto the wire rack to cool in the pan for about 5 minutes.
8. Carefully, remove from the muffin cups and place onto the wire rack to cool completely.

Dove's Cove Potatoes

Prep Time: 25 min
Total Time: 50 mins

Servings per Recipe: 10
Calories 226.3
Fat 6.6g
Cholesterol 19.0mg
Sodium 75.2mg
Carbohydrates 37.0g
Protein 5.7g

Ingredients

4 -5 large potatoes, peeled
3 large onions, sliced
4 tbsp butter
1/2 C. flour
2 C. milk
salt and pepper

Directions

1. Set your oven to 350 degrees F before doing anything else and grease a baking dish.
2. In a pan of the boiling water, cook the potatoes till halfway done.
3. Cut the potatoes into 1/4-inch thick slices and keep aside.
4. In a skillet, melt the butter and sauté the onions till transparent.
5. Sprinkle the flour on top and sauté till the flour begins to darken a little.
6. Add the milk and cook till desired consistency, stirring continuously.
7. Stir in the sliced potatoes, salt and pepper and transfer into the prepared baking dish.
8. Cook in the oven till the top becomes golden brown.

TENNESSEE
Tilapia

🥣 Prep Time: 2 mins
🕐 Total Time: 22 mins

Servings per Recipe: 5
Calories   71.7
Fat   2.6g
Cholesterol   22.6mg
Sodium   25.7mg
Carbohydrates   3.0g
Protein   9.6g

Ingredients

1/2 pint cherry tomatoes
4 garlic cloves, minced
2 tsp extra virgin olive oil
2 tbsp pesto sauce
1 lemon

2 (4 oz.) tilapia fillets
salt and pepper
Garnish
lemon wedge

Directions

1. Set your oven to 425 degrees F before doing anything else.
2. In a bowl, add the tomatoes, garlic, olive oil and a little salt and pepper and gently, mix.
3. Transfer the mixture into a baking sheet and cook in the oven for about 10 minutes.
4. In a bowl, add some of the lemon juice and pesto and mix well.
5. Season the tilapia fillets with the salt and pepper.
6. Spread the pesto mixture over the top of each tilapia fillet.
7. Cut the juiced lemon halves in half again.
8. Arrange 4 lemon pieces onto a baking sheet.
9. Place each fillet over 2 lemon pieces.
10. Cook in the oven for about 10 minutes.
11. Place 1 fillet in each serving plates.
12. Divide the tomato mixture in both plates.
13. Serve alongside the lemon wedges.

BBQ Sirloin
Nashville Style

🥣 Prep Time: 15 min
🕐 Total Time: 60 mins

Servings per Recipe: 4
Calories   247.5
Fat   7.7g
Cholesterol   75.6mg
Sodium   801.1mg
Carbohydrates   18.1g
Protein   26.1g

Ingredients
1 onion (chopped)
1 tbsp butter
1 tbsp prepared mustard
1 tbsp Worcestershire sauce
1 tbsp distilled white vinegar
2 tbsp brown sugar

1/2 tsp salt
1/2 tsp ground black pepper
1/2 C. catsup
1 lb sirloin, cut into cubes

Directions
1. In a large skillet, melt the butter on medium heat and sauté the onions till tender.
2. Add the meat and cook till browned completely.
3. Stir in the mustard, Worcestershire sauce, vinegar, salt, pepper, sugar and catsup.
4. Reduce the heat and simmer, covered for about 45 minutes, stirring occasionally.

CATFISH
Lunch Box

🥣 Prep Time: 10 mins
🕐 Total Time: 40 mins

Servings per Recipe: 5
Calories 426.5
Fat 9.8g
Cholesterol 91.0mg
Sodium 231.7mg
Carbohydrates 61.0g
Protein 24.2g

Ingredients
1 - 2 lb. catfish nuggets
1 egg
2 C. buttermilk
3 C. cornmeal
salt and pepper
oil

Directions
1. In a large bowl, add the egg and with a fork, beat well.
2. Add the buttermilk and beat till well combined.
3. In another large bowl, mix together the cornmeal, salt and pepper.
4. Rinse the nuggets.
5. Dip the nuggets into the milk mixture and then coat with the cornmeal mixture evenly.
6. In a skillet, add the enough oil that reaches halfway up.
7. Heat the oil on medium-high heat and fry the nuggets for about 3 minutes.
8. Flip the side and fry for about 2-3 minutes.

Tennessee Mac and Cheese

🥣 Prep Time: 20 min
🕐 Total Time: 50 mins

Servings per Recipe: 8
Calories 832.2
Fat 51.6g
Cholesterol 196.5mg
Sodium 1166.6mg
Carbohydrates 53.2g
Protein 38.2g

Ingredients

- 16 oz. large elbow macaroni
- 1 lb cheddar cheese
- 8 oz. monterey jack cheese
- 8 oz. Velveeta cheese
- 2 eggs
- 2 1/2 C. milk
- 1/2 C. real butter
- 2 tsp all-purpose flour
- 1/4 tsp salt
- 2 tsp black pepper
- 2 tsp olive oil

Directions

1. In a large pan of the boiling water, cook the macaroni with oil till tender.
2. Meanwhile, shred the cheddar cheese and the Monterey Jack cheese and place onto separate plates.
3. Cut the Velveeta cheese into the chunks.
4. In a bowl, add the milk, eggs, salt, pepper, flour and melted butter and mix till well combined.
5. Drain the macaroni and rinse under the cold water.
6. Place the macaroni into a large baking dish.
7. Add about half of the cheddar cheese, all of the Monterey Jack cheese and Velveeta cheese chunks in the baking dish and mix well.
8. Place the milk and egg mixture over the macaroni and mix well.
9. Sprinkle with the remaining cheddar cheese evenly.
10. Cook in the oven for about 30 minutes.

HOW TO MAKE
Collard Greens

 Prep Time: 25 mins
Total Time: 3 h 25 mins

Servings per Recipe: 6
Calories 102.7
Fat 11.4g
Cholesterol 10.8mg
Sodium 17.1mg
Carbohydrates 0.0g
Protein 0.0g

Ingredients
4 bunches collard greens
1/3 C. butter
1/2 C. chicken broth
salt and pepper
2 pinches sugar

Directions
1. Fill a large sink with cold water.
2. Place the greens for about 20 minutes.
3. Carefully, remove the greens from the sink and rinse under running cold water.
4. Tear the greens into pieces, discarding the thick veins and stems.
5. In a large pan, heat the butter on medium-high heat and cook the greens for about 2 minutes, tossing continuously.
6. Stir in the broth, salt, pepper and sugar and simmer, covered for about 3-6 hours.

Sweet Onions and Okra

Prep Time: 5 min
Total Time: 25 mins

Servings per Recipe: 6
Calories   39.9
Fat   0.2g
Cholesterol   0.0mg
Sodium   8.0mg
Carbohydrates   9.0g
Protein   1.8g

Ingredients
1 1/2 C. sweet onions, chopped
2 1/2 C. okra, sliced
3 medium tomatoes, chopped
salt & freshly ground black pepper
hot sauce

Directions
1. In a Dutch oven, add all the ingredients except the salt and pepper on medium heat and cook till desired doneness of the onion and okra.
2. Stir in the salt and pepper and serve.

BLACK Bean Shoe Peg Salad

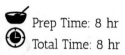

Prep Time: 8 hr
Total Time: 8 hr

Servings per Recipe: 15
Calories   247.0
Fat   12.8g
Cholesterol   0.0mg
Sodium   1219.2mg
Carbohydrates   29.7g
Protein   6.9g

Ingredients

2 (15 7/8 oz.) cans black-eyed peas, drained
2 (10 oz.) cans shoe peg corn
2 (10 oz.) cans Ro-Tel tomatoes, drained
1 (15 7/8 oz.) cans black olives, chopped
1 green pepper, chopped really small
1 red pepper, chopped really small
1 (15 7/8 oz.) cans black beans, drained
1 larger purple onion, chopped really small
3 ripe tomatoes, chopped small
1 tsp garlic powder
1 tsp onion powder
1 tsp cumin
1 tsp chili powder
1 tsp parsley flakes
16 oz. house Italian dressing

Directions

1. In a large bowl, add all the ingredients and mix well.
2. Refrigerate for at least 8 hours before serving.

Fresh Blueberry Iced Tea

Prep Time: 5 min
Total Time: 17 mins

Servings per Recipe: 1
Calories	1111.4
Fat	1.9g
Cholesterol	0.0mg
Sodium	22.1mg
Carbohydrates	285.7g
Protein	4.3g

Ingredients
4 C. fresh blueberries, rinsed and drained
2 C. water
1 C. sugar

Directions
1. In a pan, add the blueberries and water and bring to a boil.
2. Reduce the heat and simmer for about 10 minutes.
3. Line a sieve with the cheesecloth and arrange over a bowl.
4. Add the blueberry mixture in the sieve and with a spoon, press gently to release the juice.
5. Discard the pulp and transfer the juice into a pan on medium heat.
6. Add the sugar and cook till the sugar dissolves completely, stirring continuously.
7. Now, bring to a boil and cook for about 2 minutes.
8. Remove from the heat and keep aside to cool.
9. Refrigerate to chill completely before serving.
10. Add 2 tbsp of the syrup in each glass of prepared iced tea and stir well.
11. Serve with a garnishing of the lemon slices.

CHICKEN TENDERS
Tennessee Style

🍲 Prep Time: 1 hr 30 mins
🕐 Total Time: 2 hr

Servings per Recipe: 6
Calories 460.7
Fat 21.5g
Cholesterol 169.3mg
Sodium 826.0mg
Carbohydrates 28.7g
Protein 36.9g

Ingredients

4 (200 g) chicken breast fillets (boneless and skinless)
1/2 C. milk
2 eggs (lightly beaten)
1 tbsp lemon juice
1 C. plain flour
2 tsp dried thyme
2 tsp rosemary
2 tsp paprika
1 tsp salt

1/2 tsp garlic powder
peanut oil (for deep frying)
Pepper Mayo
1 C. mayonnaise
1/2 C. sour cream
2 spring onions (finely chopped)
1 tbsp green peppercorn (crushed)
1 tbsp chives
2 tsp capers (finely chopped)
tsp French mustard

Directions

1. Cut the chicken fillets into long strips.
2. In a bowl, add the milk and chicken strips and keep aside for about 1 hour.
3. Meanwhile for the mayonnaise in a bowl, add all the ingredients and mix till well combined.
4. Refrigerate till using.
5. Drain the chicken strips, reserving the milk.
6. In the bowl of the milk, add the eggs and lemon juice and beat till well combined.
7. In another bowl, mix together the flour, spices and salts.
8. Coat the chicken strips with the seasoned flour evenly.
9. Now, dip in the egg mixture and then again, coat with the seasoned flour.
10. In a deep fryer, heat the oil and fry the chicken strips in batches till golden brown.
11. With a slotted spoon, transfer the chicken strips onto a paper towel lined plate to drain.
12. Serve alongside the mayonnaise.

How to Make Black-Eyed Peas

Prep Time: 15 min
Total Time: 1 hr 45 mins

Servings per Recipe: 6
Calories 143.3
Fat 1.5g
Cholesterol 0.0mg
Sodium 124.4mg
Carbohydrates 24.0g
Protein 10.2g

Ingredients
1 lb frozen black-eyed peas
1 lb smoked turkey drumsticks
1 C. chopped onion
32 oz. low chicken broth
3 C. water
3 garlic cloves, chopped
3 tbsp pickled jalapeños chilies, chopped
salt and pepper

Directions
1. In a Dutch oven, add the peas, chicken stock, water, onions and ham hocks and bring to a boil.
2. Reduce the heat and simmer, covered for about 1 hour.
3. Stir in the chopped garlic and jalapeño chilies and simmer, covered for about 30 minutes.
4. Stir in the salt and pepper and remove from the heat.
5. Discard the ham hocks and serve.

SIMPLY
Corn Fried

🥣 Prep Time: 15 mins
🕐 Total Time: 33 mins

Servings per Recipe: 4
Calories   229.0
Fat   9.1g
Cholesterol   16.8mg
Sodium   294.6mg
Carbohydrates   33.3g
Protein   8.3g

Ingredients
6 medium fresh ears of corn
2 slices turkey bacon
1 medium yellow onion, chopped
1/2 C. red peppers, chopped
1 tsp all-purpose flour
1/4 tsp salt
1/8 tsp black pepper
1/2 C. evaporated milk

Directions
1. Cut the kernels off fresh corn. Measure 3 C. corn.
2. Heat a 10-inch non-stick on medium heat and cook the bacon till crisp.
3. With a slotted spoon, transfer the bacon onto a paper towel lined plate to drain and then crumble it.
4. Reserve the grease into the skillet.
5. In the same skillet, add the corn, onion and red pepper on medium heat and sauté for about 8 minutes, stirring continuously.
6. Stir in the flour, salt, black pepper and milk and cook for about 2 minutes, stirring continuously.
7. Serve with a sprinkling of the bacon pieces.

Buttermilk Cornbread

Prep Time: 10 min
Total Time: 1 hr

Servings per Recipe: 12
Calories   125.3
Fat   4.3g
Cholesterol   43.9mg
Sodium   266.7mg
Carbohydrates   17.2g
Protein   4.6g

Ingredients
- 1/3 C. sifted flour
- 1 1/2 C. sifted cornmeal
- 1 tsp baking soda
- 1/2 tsp salt, if desired
- 2 eggs
- 1 C. buttermilk
- 2 C. whole milk
- 1 1/2 tbsp butter

Directions
1. Set your oven to 350 degrees F before doing anything else.
2. In a bowl, sift together the flour, cornmeal, baking soda and salt.
3. In another bowl, add the eggs and beat till foamy.
4. Add the beaten eggs into the flour mixture and stir to combine.
5. Add the buttermilk and 1 C. of the whole milk and stir to combine.
6. In a 9X2-inch black skillet, melt the butter completely.
7. Immediately add the flour mixture and stir to combine.
8. Carefully, place the remaining 1 C. of the whole milk over the mixture, without stirring.
9. Transfer the skillet in the oven and cook for about 50 minutes.
10. Remove from the oven and cut into desired sized wedges before serving.

CHICKASAW
Greens

Prep Time: 10 mins
Total Time: 1 hr 10 mins

Servings per Recipe: 3
Calories 161.8
Fat 8.8g
Cholesterol 8.1mg
Sodium 997.1mg
Carbohydrates 19.4g
Protein 2.7g

Ingredients
2 lb. turnips (3 to 4 with roots)
4 C. water
1 tsp salt
2 tbsp butter

Directions
1. Cut the turnip leaves from the turnip root.
2. Wash the turnip greens under cold water completely.
3. Cut off the stem sections and then chop into small pieces.
4. Peel the turnip root and cut into small cubes.
5. In a large pan of the boiling water, cook the turnip greens, cubed roots, salt and bacon drippings and simmer for about 1 hour.
6. Serve warm.

Real Southern Macaroni and Cheese

Prep Time: 10 min
Total Time: 1 hr 5 mins

Servings per Recipe: 6
Calories   561 kcal
Fat   33.3 g
Carbohydrates   36.5 g
Protein   28.3 g
Cholesterol   100 mg
Sodium   1194 mg

Ingredients

- 2 tbsps butter
- 1/4 C. finely diced onion
- 2 tbsps all-purpose flour
- 2 C. milk
- 3/4 tsp salt
- 1/2 tsp dry mustard
- 1/4 tsp ground black pepper
- 1 (8 oz.) package elbow macaroni
- 2 C. shredded sharp Cheddar cheese
- 1 (8 oz.) package processed American cheese, cut into strips

Directions

1. Set your oven to 350 degrees before doing anything else.
2. Boil your pasta for 9 mins in water and salt. Then remove all the liquids.
3. Stir fry your onions in butter for 4 mins then add the flour and cook the mix for 20 more secs while mixing.
4. Now add in: pepper, milk, mustard, and salt.
5. Continue to heat and stir, until everything starts boiling and becomes thick.
6. Once the sauce has become thick add in the cheese and cook the sauce until the cheese melts, while continuing to stir.
7. Add the pasta to the sauce, stir the mix once, and then pour everything into a casserole dish.
8. Cook the contents in the oven for 35 mins.
9. Enjoy.

RED WHITE AND BLUE
Patty

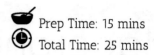
Prep Time: 15 mins
Total Time: 25 mins

Servings per Recipe: 3
Calories   691 kcal
Fat   44.2 g
Carbohydrates   35.4g
Protein   37.3 g
Cholesterol   129 mg
Sodium   1574 mg

Ingredients
1 lb ground beef
3 tbsps chili seasoning mix
2 chipotle peppers in adobo sauce, minced
1/4 C. mayonnaise
1 chipotle pepper in adobo sauce, minced
6 (1 oz.) slices white bread
6 (1/2 oz.) slices pepperjack cheese

Directions
1. Get a bowl, combine: adobo sauce, ground beef, 2 chipotle peppers, and chili seasoning.
2. Now, with your hands, form three burgers from the mix.
3. Get a 2nd bowl, combine: 1 chipotle pepper and the mayo.
4. Coat your pieces of bread with this mix, and add a piece of cheese.
5. Now fry your burgers for 6 mins per side then place them on top of the cheese.
6. Place another piece of bread to from a burger.
7. Remove some of the drippings from the pan and, for 2 mins, fry each side of the burger in the hot drippings.
8. Enjoy.

Easy Jalapeno Bites

Prep Time: 1 hr
Total Time: 1 hr 20 mins

Servings per Recipe: 20
Calories   189 kcal
Fat   18.2 g
Carbohydrates   2g
Protein   < 4.6 g
Cholesterol   40 mg
Sodium   256 mg

Ingredients

- 2 (12 oz.) packages ground sausage
- 2 (8 oz.) packages cream cheese, softened
- 30 jalapeno chili peppers, cut in half horizontally, seeds taken out
- 1 lb sliced turkey bacon, cut in half

Directions

1. Set your oven to 375 degrees before doing anything else.
2. Stir fry your sausage until fully done then place them in a bowl with the cream cheese.
3. Fill your pieces of pepper with the sausage mix and then wrap bacon around each one.
4. Place the contents into a casserole dish and cook everything in the oven for 24 mins.
5. Enjoy.

PINTO BEANS
Tennessee

Prep Time: 15 mins
Total Time: 2 h 15 mins

Servings per Recipe: 8
Calories   210 kcal
Fat   1.1 g
Carbohydrates   37.9 g
Protein   13.2 g
Cholesterol   1 mg
Sodium   < 95 mg

Ingredients

- 1 lb dry pinto beans
- 1 (29 oz.) can reduced sodium chicken broth
- 1 large onion, diced
- 1 fresh jalapeno pepper, diced
- 2 cloves garlic, minced
- 1/2 C. green salsa
- 1 tsp cumin
- 1/2 tsp ground black pepper
- water, if needed

Directions

1. Get the following boiling: pepper, beans, cumin, broth, onions, salsa, jalapenos, and garlic.
2. Let the contents cook for 2 hrs.
3. If the mix gets too dry add some water and continue cooking for the remaining time.
4. Enjoy.

Sweet Honey Chicken

Prep Time: 10 mins
Total Time: 1 hr 45 mins

Servings per Recipe: 4
Calories 481 kcal
Fat 21.5 g
Carbohydrates 49.4g
Protein 22.8 g
Cholesterol 65 mg
Sodium 6378 mg

Ingredients

- 3 C. cold water
- 1/4 C. kosher salt
- 1/4 C. honey
- 4 boneless skinless chicken breast halves
- 1/4 C. buttermilk
- 1 C. all-purpose flour
- 1 tsp black pepper
- 1/2 tsp garlic salt
- 1/2 tsp onion salt
- cayenne pepper to taste
- vegetable oil for frying

Directions

1. Get a bowl, combine: honey, water, and salt.
2. Now place the chicken in the water (make sure the liquid covers the chicken).
3. Place a covering of plastic wrap around the bowl and chill the mix in the fridge for 2 hrs.
4. Now put your chicken in another bowl and cover it with buttermilk.
5. Let the chicken stand for 30 mins in the milk.
6. Add your veggie oil to a frying and pan and begin heating it to 350 degrees before doing anything else.
7. Now get a 3rd bowl, mix: cayenne, flour, onion salt, garlic salt, and black pepper.
8. Dredge your chicken in the dry mix then fry it for 13 mins per side in the hot oil
9. Enjoy.

AUTHENTIC
Southern Corn

Prep Time: 10 mins
Total Time: 20 mins

Servings per Recipe: 6	
Calories	359 kcal
Fat	22.7 g
Carbohydrates	38.2g
Protein	8 g
Cholesterol	61 mg
Sodium	491 mg

Ingredients
2 (15.25 oz.) cans whole kernel corn, drained
1 (8 oz.) package cream cheese
1/4 C. butter
10 jalapeno peppers, diced
1 tsp garlic salt

Directions
1. Cook the following for 15 mins, in a large, pot: garlic salt, corn, jalapenos, butter, and cream cheese.
2. Stir the mix every 2 to 3 mins.
3. Enjoy.

American
Dinner Rolls

🥣 Prep Time: 12 mins
🕐 Total Time: 35 mins

Servings per Recipe: 12
Calories   202
Fat   11.1g
Cholesterol   26mg
Sodium   368mg
Carbohydrates   18.4g
Fiber   1.5g
Protein   6.4g

Ingredients
1 C. Parmesan cheese, grated freshly
½ C. butter, melted
1 (1 lb.) frozen bread dough loaf, cut into 36 equal pieces

Directions
1. Grease 12 cups of a large-sized muffin tin.
2. Divide grated cheese in prepared muffin cups evenly.
3. In a bowl, add melted butter.
4. With your hands, roll each piece of dough in a ball shape.
5. Then dip the dough balls in melted butter completely.
6. Place 3 balls in each muffin cup and gently, press down the balls in cheese.
7. Cover the muffin cups with a light cloth. Keep in warm place for about 5-7 ours.
8. Set your oven to 375 degrees F.
9. Bake for about 20-25 minutes or till golden brown.

ENJOY THE RECIPES?
KEEP ON COOKING WITH 6 MORE FREE COOKBOOKS!

Visit our website and simply enter your email address to join the club and receive your 6 cookbooks.

http://booksumo.com/magnet

 https://www.instagram.com/booksumopress/

 https://www.facebook.com/booksumo/